everybody dies....

and that's okay

# everybody dies....

# and that's okay

written & illustrated
by
peacewillow devine

everybody dies....and that's okay

ISBN 979-8-218-84415-8

bisac SOC036000
science/death & dying


first paperback edition june 2025


published by peacewillow's perspective
www.peacewillowsperspective.com


printed in the usa

# table of contents

(3)

(4)

# chapter

# one

# why
# Death
# happens

(6)

does the thought of death
sadden or scare you?

while most people consider
the loss of anyone to be a
tragedy, death is really just
a necessary part of life.

as a matter of fact,
without the death and
evolution cycle of life on
earth, humans would not
even exist....

(8)

nature needed to go thru
the creation and destruction
of trilobites, blastoids,
spiny sharks and therapsids,
among others,
before the first mammal
even appeared on this planet,
and it was close to another
200 million years before that
little rodent spawned
our more direct ancestors,
of which there were many.

if not for death, homo sapiens
might be sharing earth with
homo erectus, neanderthals, and
denisovans, along with all the
other "human" species who have
ever existed, not to mention all
the dinosaurs!!

which brings us to the practical
issue of space for everyone....
not to mention resources, like
food and water.

(9)

# earth has had
## 5 major extinctions....

**1. ordovician-silurian @443.8 mya**
71-85% of life wiped out

**2. late devonian @372 mya**
70-75% of life wiped out

**3. permian-triassic (the great dying)**
@252 million years ago
80-96% of marine life and
70% of land species wiped out

**4. late triassic @200 mya**
76-80% of life wiped out

**5. cretaceous-paleogene @66 mya**
67-75% of life wiped out

only one species survived all 5 extinctions:
the tiny tardigrades, aka water bears!

nature has a way of
regulating those types
of things, with reproduction
dropping off if resources
become tight, but then a
community will stagnate,
since each new generation
brings new mutations,
new ways of surviving and new
strengths to the species.


death is a way to encourage
new growth and new
experiences,
which is why it was built into
the circle of life....


you're born, you live, you die,
and then you repeat that over
and over again in different
forms.

(12)

see, at its core,
everything that exists
is simply made up
of energy,
of atoms, and sub-atomic
particles, and whatever
smaller bits scientists have
found.

when a physical body dies,
whether a tree, or
a squirrel,
or a human, those atoms are
released as the body decays,
sending that energy back
out into the universe
to be reused in
something new.

and that's pretty awesome, if
you think about it....

(14)

nature designed all life
with an expiration date,
to make sure
that energy exchange
kept going,
creating new life
and new experiences thru
millions and millions
of years.


of course, that expiration
date varies wildly,
with some creatures
only living for a day or two,
while others may get
hundreds, or thousands,
of years in one body.

but the amount of time
you get isn't as important
as what you do
with that time
while you're here.

(16)

the vast majority
of creatures on earth
have no knowledge of
their own mortality, so they
just live life.

while they are smart enough to
avoid danger, when possible,
and they recognize when a
friend fails to do so,
they don't anticipate or
fear their end, like so many
humans do.

the human ego -
that "big brain" we
all love so much -
is highly aware that
someday it will cease
to exist as it is right now,
and that thought
is absolutely terrifying to most
human minds.

(18)

but it is extremely important to recognize that fear as irrational, since death is not something anyone can avoid, and there's no point in fearing the inevitable.

it would be better to try to see the gift inherent in each new day, no matter how miserable your life may seem at the moment.

knowing that this life, with all its hardships, joys and possibilities, is simply a temporary state of being can help you to free your mind of all those "oh so serious" thoughts, plans, emotions and fears that stress you out so much.

live each day as if it's your last one, because someday it will be.

you were designed that way.

(20)

# chapter two

∞

# how
# Death
# happens

(22)

at this point, you may
be wondering how, exactly,
nature's imposed expiration
date works, so let's talk
about what keeps you alive.

with the exception of single
celled organisms, every
living being is made up of
other miniature lifeforms
called cells.

each cell in a body has a
specific job to do, and each
one has its own expiration date,
but they also have a trick....

they can replicate
themselves so that their
"children" can continue the
work without
any interruption of services,
for a while, at least.

life cycle of a random cell

(24)

as with all life, tho, the cells can only reproduce themselves so many times, and each reproduction cycle offers the chance for a deadly mutation, like cancer, to occur, throwing off the entire system.

even running smoothly, with no issues to speak of, the cells will start to slow down, and then cease reproduction altogether at some point, leading to breakdowns in the body, often starting with a lower immune system, which can then allow in other organisms, some with ill intent.

while there are things you, as a human, can do to help keep your cells healthy and living their best lives, you must also understand that they will die eventually, just like every other living being.

try to think
about your pace,
'cause slow and steady
wins the race!

as for how long you
and your cells might have,
well, that's a mystery.

some scientists opine that
heartbeats are a way to
measure a lifespan, for some
creatures, anyway.

they note that a mouse,
with a resting heartbeat of
500-700 bpm, only has
a life expectancy of 1-3 years,
while a galapagos tortoise,
with just 6 bpm on average,
has been known to live
177 years or more, which
may be a reminder to watch
that stress level....

of course, some of the oldest
known beings on earth don't
even have heartbeats, at least,
not ones that we can hear,
whether we're talking about
sponges, coral or a 5,000 year old
bristlecone pine tree.

# EXTREME
## EXPIRATION DATES

if your only purpose on earth
is to reproduce, then life can be
very short, indeed:
adult mayflies = 5 mins-24 hours
luna moths = 1 week
mosquitoes = 2 weeks
**shortest lived mammal**
commom shrew = 1 year

but, if you have a much slower
metabolism and just want to hang out
for awhile, you could get some time:
black coral = 5,000 years
antarctic moss = 5,500 years
deep-sea sponges = 11,000 years
**longest lived mammal**
bowhead whales = 200 years

even the so-called
"immortal jellyfish" (t.dohrnii),
who can allegedly regenerate
themselves indefinitely,
are, unfortunately for them,
very tasty food sources for
bigger creatures, meaning it's
rare for immortality to ever
become reality for them.

which, of course, brings us to the
point of how many creatures
actually reach the expiration date
that nature had set for them.

some people would say none,
since "old age" is rarely listed as
a cause of death for anyone
anymore, but that's more about
semantics than anything.

it is the condition of your cells
that matters, and nothing else.

as your cells slow down
and start to deteriorate
due to old age, outside
bacteria, viruses and disease
can slip in, and those
are usually named
as the causes of death,
which can be misleading.

because cells can be
injured, and killed off,
in so many different ways,
it's no surprise that medical
professionals  have come up
with  literally thousands
of causes of death.

even something as simple
as your heart stops
beating in your sleep will be
described as some sort of
avoidable heart disease,
rather than the
natural end of life that it is.

(31)

time spent
sniffing flowers
is never
wasted time!

peacewillow
·7/12/11

(32)

yes, your behavior
absolutely does have
an effect on your cells'
ability to do their jobs,
but nothing you do
will expand that
expiration date
or stop death from
coming for you.

does that mean you
shouldn't take care
of yourself, since
you're gonna die anyway?

of course not!

it's not the quantity of life that
matters; it's the quality.

let's say your expiration date
is age 65......

(33)

dance

(34)

if you want to have an
active, healthy and happy life
till the day you die, preferably at
your latest possible expiration
date, you'll need to start taking
care of yourself in your 20s,
with exercise, healthy eating and a
fairly stress-free lifestyle.

you could even have some fun
in your 20s and start healthy living
in your 30s or 40s, but you
can't expect your body to be in
good shape at its end if you didn't
bother to care for it at its peak.

in the end, the only person
who will really pay for your
lack of self care is you, because
death comes in many forms,
and sometimes the process
seems to last for years,
which can be quite painful,
for everyone involved....

(36)

# chapter three

∞

# when Death happens

it can be a real
eat or be eaten
kind of world
out there...

but sometimes
it's just playtime!

(38)

while it would be nice if
every being was able to live
a healthy life to its natural
expiration date, that's just not
how things work in reality.

most creatures live their
entire lives under
the specter of death,
whether they know it or not,
simply because they are
considered to be food by
someone else....

but even those at the
top of the food chain are
subject to injury, disease,
natural disasters and human
destruction.

because of these variables,
death can actually happen
to anyone, at any time,
without warning.

the loss of a dream

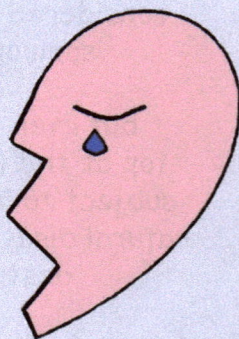

is the worst loss there is

(40)

if a child dies before
actually being born,
they call it a miscarriage or
stillbirth, but making it out of
the womb alive doesn't
guarantee anything.

death before age 5 is a very
real possibility, mainly due to
the immune system not being up
to the fight against the many
diseases vying to enter the
new body, along with any
developmental issues that
may exist.

if you can make it thru all of
that, you open yourself up to
fatal injuries from accidents,
like drowning and car crashes,
which are the leading causes of
death for those ages 5-18,
unless you live in the united
states, where firearms are now
the leading cause of death for
that age range....

(41)

when all
else fails....

simply blend in with your
surroundings!

(42)

altho, to be fair,
by the time you reach
adulthood, violence, of one
sort or another, jumps in to
the mix of possible causes of
death for every species on
every continent.

as a matter of fact,
it's fair to say that humans
prevent a good number of beings
from reaching their natural
expiration dates, but that's
probably a subject for a
different book....

suffice it to say that many
circumstances determine when
death happens, and no one has
control over all of them.

while a critter can certainly
make an effort to avoid being
eaten, a tree cannot sidestep
a chainsaw.

(43)

**death**
is just a
reminder.....

...*that life is a*
*temporary*
*state of being.*

(44)

keeping your body
strong does, however,
encourage quick recovery
from any mishaps that may
occur, as long as you
understand that it's not a
guarantee of anything.

the phrase "it was just
their time to go" is often said
when death is the result
of some freak accident, or
sudden, unexplained,
medical emergency, and
it's an apt assessment
of the event,
altho others may say
"they were taken before their
time", which is subjective, at
best.

for those who make it to
the designated "middle age",
it may feel like everything
is out to get you, but that's
only half true.

dear children of earth,
please try to understand...

you are responsible
for the state of your world.
what you watch on tv,
what you buy with your money,
how you feel about yourself,
what you put into your body,
how you treat other creatures,
what you consider important...
all of this creates the world
we all live in.
please be more mindful....

(46)

this is where your own
body care, or lack thereof,
comes back to haunt you.

if you have not kept your
body in good physical condition,
you may start having balance
and strength issues, causing
injuries, or even death, from
falls in your own home.

there's also a good chance that
all those years of drug or
alcohol abuse, along with poor
eating habits, have caused
unseen issues within your body,
which will now start surfacing as
diabetes, heart disease,
cirrhosis, or cancer, among
other things.

but, even if you made a point to
eat well, and never smoked,
drank alcohol or consumed any
recreational drugs in your entire
life, you're still not safe.

(47)

since the
"plastics revolution"
first began in the 1950s,
over 8.3 billion metric tons
of the stuff has been
produced, and it
doesn't go away.
microplastics are found
in the air we breathe,
the water we drink,
the soil our food grows in
and inside every living thing on
earth, including us.

and they are not harmless.

microplastics found in human
blood, lungs, liver & kidneys
cause respiratory problems,
organ damage, neurotoxicity,
cancer, endocrine disruption,
issues within your
intestinal microbiome, and
can even increase the risk of
heart attacks and strokes.....

the past 150 years or so
have seen levels of
human created pollution
skyrocket planetwide,
forcing every living being to
ingest coal soot, asbestos,
microplastics, and a myriad
of deadly chemicals, every day
of their lives.

the water we all drink,
the air we all breathe,
the soil in which our food grows,
as well as our food itself.....

all of it is contaminated,
and those chemicals
are absolutely affecting
our bodies from the moment
of conception, as a newborn
infant has hundreds of
chemicals in their bloodstream,
even before taking their
first breath.

(50)

in the most practical
sense, death happens when
your cells can no longer
maintain life,
whether due to injury,
mutations, disease, or age.


of course, all of that goes
out the window when someone
chooses to deliberately
end their own life,
no matter the condition
of their body.


suicide demonstrates both
a lack of compassion for
the self, and a tragic
misunderstanding of what the
purpose of life truly is....


to simply live, no matter the
circumstances.

(51)

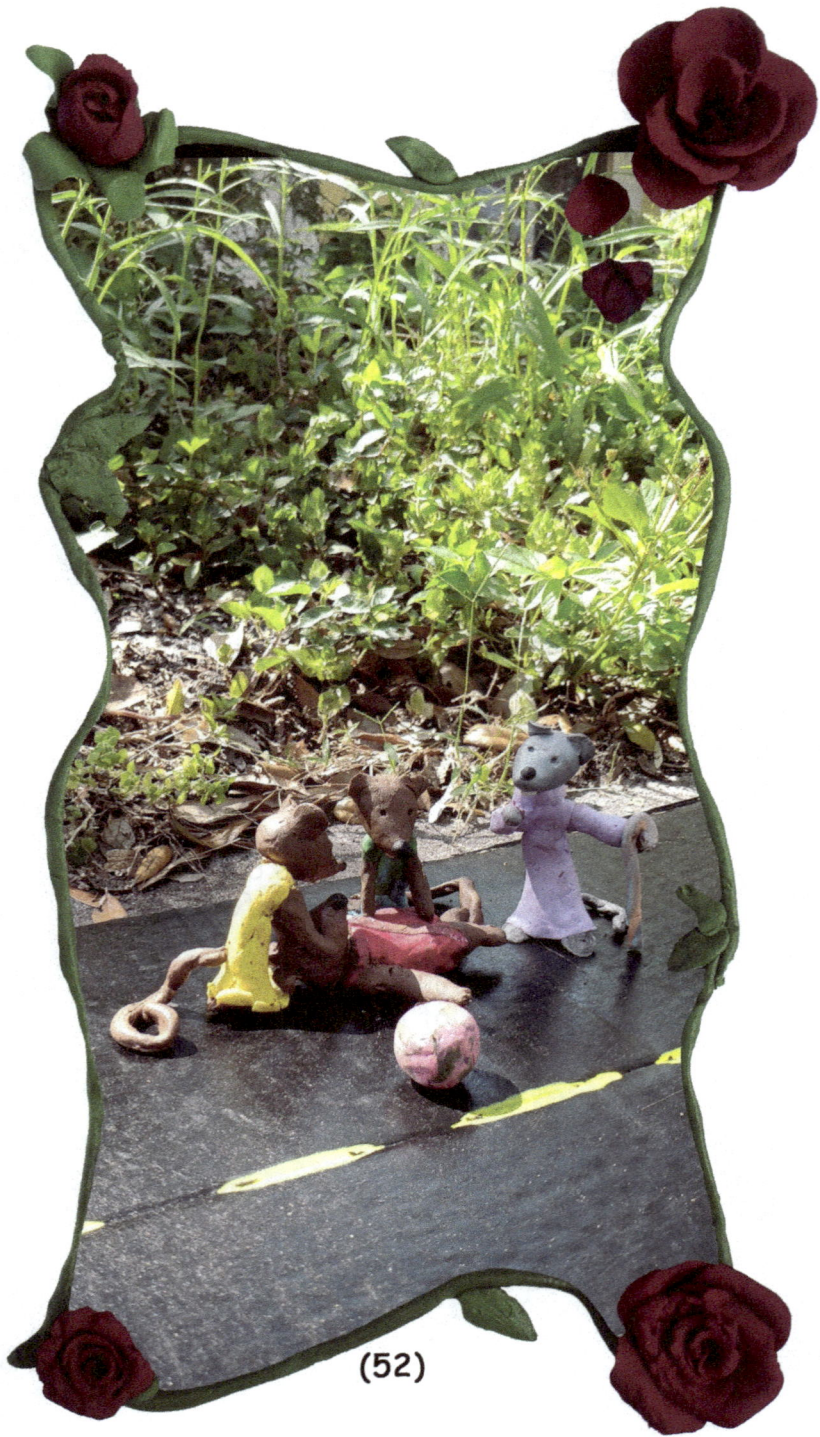

(52)

# chapter four

∞

# where Death happens

# top 10 causes of death (worldwide)

1. coronary heart disease
2. stroke
3. copd (chronic obstructive pulmonary disease)
4. lower respiratory tract infection
5. alzheimer's/dementia
6. cancers of the lungs, trachea and bronchus
7. diabetes complications
8. road injury (accident)
9. diarrheal diseases
10. tuberculosis

**lack of physical activity can increase the risk of chronic illnesses, so keep moving until you can't anymore!!**

where a being dies is
very much tied in to how
and when their last
breath arrives.

with most fatal
accidents and violent attacks,
death occurs at that scene,
whether at home, in traffic,
in the water, or inside a
public building of some sort,
even tho death will most
likely be declared later,
in a hospital.

however, as horrendous as
those causes are, they
do not represent the
majority of human deaths,
with less than 10% of
the world's adult population
succumbing to accidents,
suicide or other violent acts.

(55)

# home is where
## the heart is....

## <u>hospice resources</u>

## www.hospice.org

over 95 countries now
offer some sort
of national
hospice or palliative care

## iahpc.org
(int'l assoc. for hospice &
palliative care)

on the other hand,
over 50% of people
worldwide will die at home,
whether alone or with
someone by their side, and
that seems like the most
natural place to die, if you
think about it.

even wild animals will try
to get home if they
know their time is near,
because home is the most
comforting place to be,
in most cases, anyway.

but, if you live in a
more developed area,
a richer nation perhaps,
you are far more likely to
die in a medical facility
of some sort, whether a
hospital or care center.

home death pros:
1. comfort, privacy and familiarity
2. reduced exposure to infections
3. low cost - 1/3 the cost of dying in a hospital

facility death pros:
1. caregivers available 24/7
2. access to specialized care
3. takes the burden of care off family and friends

** ultimately, the patient's preferences and wishes should be the primary consideration, if that is at all possible. **

(58)

the main reason for
this is wealthier communities
having the ability to access
modern medical treatments,
along with the ongoing care
necessary to alleviate the
symptoms and pain associated
with long-term
medical issues, which plague
some people for years,
or even decades,
before death finally
comes for them.

the one good thing about
dying in a facility is
that someone will know
pretty much right away,
unlike if you live alone
and die of a heart attack
in your sleep.....
altho that may only be a problem
for whoever finds you!

# checklist for the dying

1. gather all important papers in one place

2. write down all account numbers and passwords

3. transfer big items to heirs before death

4. write down final wishes (burial, cremation, etc)

5. give special possessions to who you want to have them

6. close any accounts that you can

7. let people know how much they meant to you

(60)

where you die can
absolutely have an effect on
the dying process itself,
as well as on the grieving
process that follows for
those in attendence.

a home death allows
for closure on many levels.

friends and family have
the opportunity to privately visit
and say good-bye without
facility restrictions, and,
if they feel up to it,
the dying person has the
opportunity to go thru things,
giving away what they want, to
whoever they want to have it,
as well as putting any paperwork
in order, all while saying anything
and everything they've
always wanted to say.

(62)

it's not always our choice,
but, if we have that choice,
it's something to think about.

however, if you do live alone,
you might wanna ask someone
to check in on you now and then,
just in case....

and you should probably do the
same for others, whether
family, friends or neighbors.

the sad truth is that over 15% of
earth's seniors (people over age 60)
live alone, with many having no family
left to miss them, and that figure
nearly doubles to 28% if you live
in a "developed" area, like
the united states or europe.

over 8 billion humans on this planet,
but the older you get, the more
likely you are to die at home alone,
and not be discovered for some time....

(64)

it's also worth noting
that "where" can refer
to more than just your
physical location.

where your mind is obviously
plays an important role in
your last act on earth,
and it definitely affects those
you leave behind.

some say that a person
knows when they are close
to death, but whether or not
they acknowledge it is up
to each individual.

if you CAN find a way
to acknowledge your
impending death without
total fear, well, you,
my friend, are a hero
with courage to spare!

just for today,
can you accept

that everything happens
for a reason?

being able to gracefully
accept the end of your life
on earth will allow you
to look back on your
adventures with gratitude,
rather than sadness
or anger, as well as allow
you to recognize whatever
mistakes need to be addressed
before leaving, if that's
something you'd like to do.

to be sure, there is no way
around the sadness of death,
for everyone involved....

but having the opportunity
to talk about the experience,
to laugh over old memories,
to say your "thank you"s,
"i love you"s and "good-bye"s,
is a blessing beyond compare,
no matter where your final
moment takes place.

(68)

# chapter five

∞

# what
# happens
# after
# Death

(70)

the moment of death
occurs when the body
ceases its earthly functioning,
and it is generally considered
to be a painless event, altho
the circumstances surrounding
it may sometimes dictate
otherwise, depending on
the cause of death.

many creatures simply
lie down, close their eyes
and just stop breathing,
altho some humans have been
known to take their last breath
mid-sentence, reminding us
that the moment of death
is not something we can
consciously control.

we can, however, control
our thoughts on the matter,
and that can make a
huge difference.

(71)

(72)

someone who is fighting
death, for whatever reason,
seems to have a more
difficult final moment than
those who have accepted
the inevitable.

whatever the case, tho,
that final breath will come to
all of us, one way or another,
and, when it does,
there are things that will
need to be done.

if you die in a hospital,
or facility of some sort,
they will generally take care
of the immediate actions that
are necessary but, if you die
at home, whoever discovers
that you have stopped breathing
will have some phone calls
to make, even before the
mind has had time to
process the death.

(73)

# after death to do list

1. order 10-12 copies of the death certificate
2. file the will
3. transfer utilities to whoever will inherit the house
4. cancel all autopays and close most accounts
5. close out all credit cards and bank accounts
6. decide who will be responsible for sorting and distributing possessions
7. take time to grieve, and ask for help, if you need it

(74)

your doctor, or 911,
depending on the time of day
and circumstances, will
need to be called to
officially declare the death
before the funeral home of
choice will be able to retrieve
the body, which is what you will
now be known as.

if hospice, or other nurses,
were involved in the end care,
they will need to be called in
to collect any narcotic
medications or bio-hazardous
materials left behind, and
a medical supply company may
also need to be called, if any
equipment needs to be returned.

in between all of this
will be the calls to family
and friends, informing them
of the death.

i can not
envision a future,
which makes it
really hard
to pull together
the energy and
motivation
needed to do
the things that
will create the path
that i will walk
into the future
i can not envision....

the first 24 hours
after a loved one
passes on are often a blur,
even if the death was anticipated.

you may seek activity, something
to physicallly do, as your mind
tries to comprehend the situation.

shock is simply your mind
freezing in place, not wanting
to deal with the loss, and that's
perfectly understandable.

it's important to try to have
that initial grieving session with
others, in order to pour out all those
pent up tears and emotions in
a safe space, before you delve into
the details to follow because,
while the deceased has no more
worries, chances are good that
they left behind a pile of
unfinished stuff, not to mention,
they still need to make it to
their final resting place.

## favorite movies about the afterlife

for the serious minded,
nothing beats 1998's
"what dreams may come",
a visually stunning depiction
of heaven as whatever you
imagine it to be.
starring robin williams

for the not so serious,
check out 1991's
"defending your life",
a quirky comedy that takes
us to judgment city after
death, where a trial will
determine whether you
overcame fear in your life.
starring albert brooks
and meryl streep

someone will need to
be designated to handle
the practicalities of death,
such as cremation or burial,
funeral or celebration of life,
written will or free for all estate....

not to mention that someone
will need to clean out, organize
and dispose of all the belongings
the deceased had spent a lifetime
collecting, and then decide
what to do with the house,
if there is one.

but maybe all that isn't
what you wanted to hear about
the after death experience.

maybe you thought this chapter
was going to be about whether or
not there is life after death....

so let's talk about that for a minute.

(80)

scientifically speaking,
we have no way of knowing
whether any part of someone
survives death, other than
those atoms we talked about
earlier, altho some near death
experiences certainly seem to hint
that something survives, if only
for a short period of time.

scientists are learning that
our cells do not all immediately
keel over dead when our body
stops maintaining our life,
but do those cells contain our
consciousness, or do they
each have their own?

if you are religious, you may
believe that our consciousness
transitions to a different plane
of existence, like heaven, but
that belief seems to be rooted
in an extreme fear of death,
and not much more.

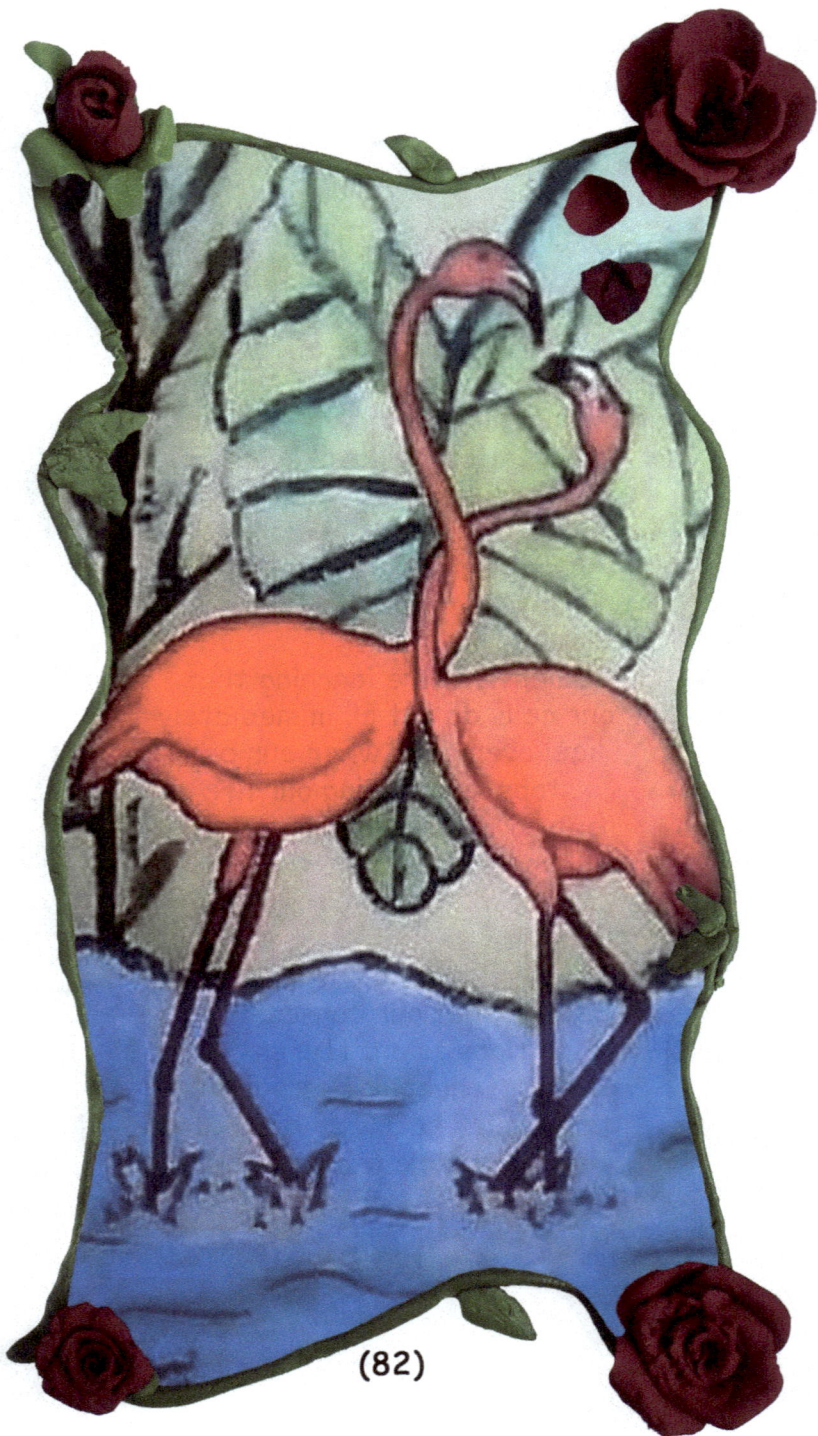

(82)

perhaps those atoms
hold memories of the life
just lived, but, even if they did,
it would be just one life of many,
as a group of atoms take on a
different character with
each new incarnation.

whether our essence
-the soul or spirit that made us US-
lives on after physical death
really shouldn't be something
we worry about, because it
doesn't matter to the life
we are living right now, and
we won't know the truth
until we die anyway.

but, if it makes us feel
better to believe that we will
see our deceased loved ones
again when we die, then there
really isn't any harm in it,
especially since we don't know
the truth either way.

(83)

(84)

# chapter six

∞

# who grieves Death

remember, you are
always right here....

lost and found

in case you forget,
as we sometimes do.

in the end,
the why, how, when,
where and what of death
don't really matter
when all you feel is the
sadness of loss.

altho everyone grieves
differently, it is generally
accepted that the closer
you were to a being,
the stronger your
grief will be.

anyone who was a part
of your daily life,
whether a pet, a child,
or a spouse, will be extremely
missed, simply because
your daily routine is disrupted
and their energy is missing
from the house.

this is why we say we feel lost
without them....

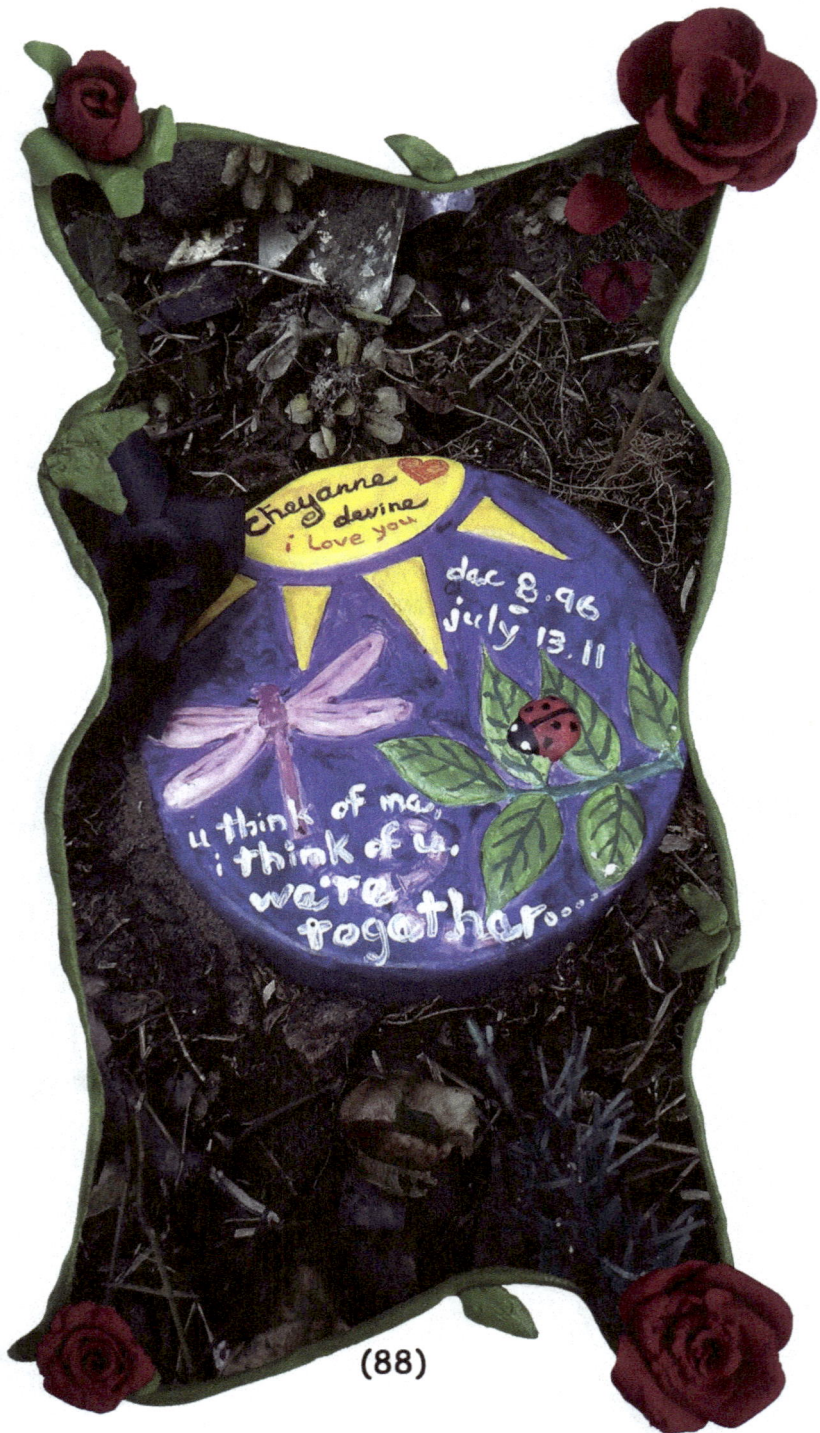

some people will choose to
immediately purge their space
of all reminders of the being,
thinking that will lessen
their grief, but putting away
that food bowl or pair of
reading glasses isn't really
gonna make you stop thinking
about them, and there's
a reason for that.....

grief is simply an intense sadness
over an irreversible loss,
and our lives are full of it,
from way more than just
physical death, which is why
it's good to learn how to navigate
thru those emotions in
a healthy way.

grief is just as necessary
to life as death is,
because the only constant
in life is change.

(89)

contrary to
popular belief....
the point of life is
not to be happy.
altho contentment is nice.

it's not about making money,
altho comfort is nice.

it's not about love
or companionship,
altho caring for others is nice.

the point of life is
to learn and
to grow,
and those two things
almost always involve
hardship and difficulty.

deal with it.

some may think that grief
is "all in your head"
but they would be mistaken.

rather than being a selfish
indulgence, true grief is,
at times, an uncontrollable
full body experience....
and not allowing for the
full expression of it can have
dire consequences for your
mental and physical well being.

refusing to acknowledge or
consciously deal with your grief
can cause a myriad of issues,
from irritability and problems
sleeping, to headaches, tummy
troubles and even heart attacks.

while it's true that grieving hurts,
ignoring it hurts more in the
long run, so be kind to yourself by
allowing the sadness now.

(91)

it's okay
to cry

in fact,
it's necessary

tears are cleansing,
literally washing toxins
from your body, so cry
as much as you need to, and
then cry some more.

you'll notice how much calmer you
feel afterwards, with each cry
becoming a little less intense
as time goes on.

and give your mind a break,
if you can, because "brain fog" is a
very real thing at times like this.

your brain is busy trying to
process the loss of a life it enjoyed
spending time with, as well as
struggling with the thought
of its own mortality,
so it's not 100% focused on
whatever you think it is,
and you need to recognize and
acknowledge that before
screwing up something important.

(93)

sometimes the pain
of missing you
feels like a hot knife
carving up my heart
and i just wanna
bang my head
against a wall
until
we're together
again....

(94)

your emotions, being
entwined with that big brain,
are also freaking out, and
maybe not expressing themselves
as clearly as they could be, which
can lead to some real craziness
if left unchecked.

professionals will tell you
that you shouldn't make any major
decisions in the first year following
a devastating loss, but rarely do
people heed that advice, often
leading to some irreversible actions
that  cause regret as time goes by.

yes, grief hurts, more than
physical injury sometimes, but
you can't hide from or bury
that grief without causing further
harm to yourself.

rather than being a sign of weakness,
facing your grief head on takes a
tremendous amount of courage.

## <u>grief resources</u>

while there are many books
available on the topic,
elisabeth kubler-ross remains
the gold standard.
1969's "on death and dying" and
1997's "the wheel of life"
are two of her best.

if you prefer videos, visit
www.youtube.com/
@jennyapple4704
where kyle appleford shares his
journey thru grief as a single father
of two young children after his
beloved wife passed away in 2023
at just 36, after a two year battle
with cancer, which she also
documented on this channel.
jenny's courage and grace while
facing the end of her life
is simply inspirational.

(96)

in addition to sadness,
it's important to note that
other emotions may make
an appearance, too, sometimes
without any specific reason.

anger is very common,
whether towards the person
who died, the doctor who
treated them, or the ailment
blamed for the death.

guilt can also rear its ugly head,
especially the first time you laugh
or feel happy after the loss.

if the death was sudden, you may
resent the fact that you didn't get
to say "good-bye" in person.....

no matter what you feel, it's fine.
try to just let the emotions
flow thru you, without holding on
to any of them in particular.

have i ever
told you
how grateful i am
to have
shared my life
with you?

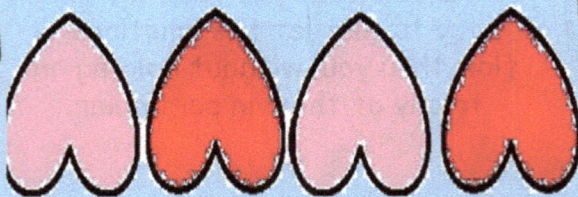

this roller coaster
of emotions is just your
mind's way of working thru
the process of grieving, trying
to find the right thought or
emotion to make the pain go away,
not realizing that time is
the only true healer.

everything that exists
on earth is only here for a
temporary time, so, if we live
long enough, we will have to adapt
to many losses and changes.

if you can learn to swim thru the
depths of grief's despair,
you will be rewarded with the gift
of beautiful memories of fun
adventures with wonderful
souls of every species.

hopefully, in time, rather
than feeling sad that they are gone,
you will simply feel grateful that
you knew them at all.

(100)

# chapter seven

∞

# legacy of Death

(102)

none of us, no matter
our species, would be who
we are without the influence
of others on our lives, for
better or for worse.

our parents often birth and
raise us, but, even if
they don't, they pass on the
fundamentals of our life
thru their dna.

as we grow up, we are often
surrounded by siblings or
cousins, learning the basics
of survival from each other
as we go along.

as adults, we choose mates,
whether long term or simple
procreation hook ups, and
we may even belong to a
group or tribe of some sort.

(103)

Wolverine

(104)

even those who
choose to live mostly
solitary lives are not isolated
from the influence of the
other species around them.

and it is that influence,
which most beings give
little or no thought to,
that is the  greatest legacy of
death, because it is what
keeps life moving forward.

without the knowledge
of how to survive,
whether supplied by
dna or taught directly
to young ones, what
species would survive at all?

(106)

for most humans, the word
"legacy" conjures up images of
vast estates, trophies, statues, or
some other physical recognition
of achievement, even though those
aren't really the important parts.

having your name on a museum
wing may seem impressive, but
what influence does it have on
those who visit the museum,
other than being able to do so?

a better memorial would be a
video or book about all of your
adventures, and all that you
learned in your lifetime, as well as
how you touched the lives
of others because of it.

in truth, you don't need to
achieve worldwide recognition
to leave a legacy, since living a life
is the only requirement for that.

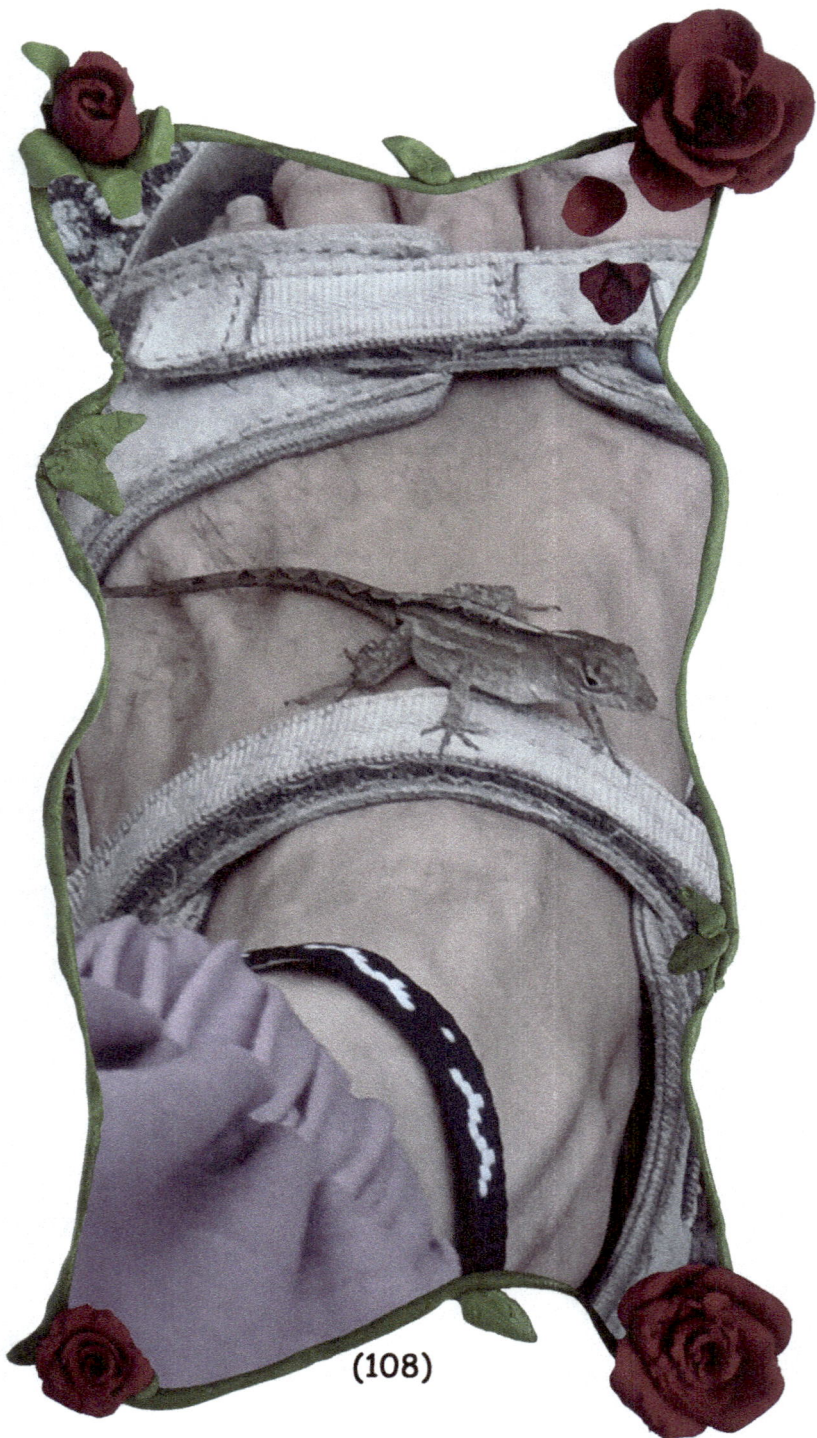

(108)

if you'd like to know what
your current legacy is,
simply look around you.

do you have children?
how you raised them is part of
your legacy, since you gave them
their foundation in life.

do you have friends?
how would they describe you
if you died right now?

what kind of job do you have?
if you are a teacher or educator
of some sort, your students reflect
your legacy by carrying
the lessons you imparted to them
into the future.

or maybe you are a social worker, or
in the medical profession, or a retail
worker who helped someone pick out
the perfect gift once....

no matter what you do, you
have an influence on others.

(109)

every morning, as i wake,
i miss you.
as i go thru my day,
walking our streets,
i miss you.
the only constant in life
is change,
we all know it's true,
but one thing
that will never change
is my love for you.

(110)

when someone leaves
our life, grief will
sometimes temporarily block
out a lot of the good stuff,
simply because it hurts
too much to think about
at that moment,
but, if you can get thru that
difficult grieving phase,
you will be rewarded with
the full memory of how much
that being actually left you,
which is why we say that they
never really leave us at all.

having photos of your
loved ones around, especially
if they depict particular
favorite moments together,
is a great way to remind
ourselves of their influence
everyday, even tho they are
no longer physically with us.

(111)

(112)

at this point, it's
important to mention that
not everyone will leave a
necessarily positive legacy
behind, but there's still helpful
lessons to be learned, even
from not so nice influences.

those who mistreat us teach
us to defend ourselves, or
find another way to survive
the encounter.

those who are hateful and
angry at the world can teach
us compassion and empathy
for the unseen pain of others.

and those who bully and tease
us can teach us to have more
confidence in ourselves,
just as we are.

remember, how we react
to others is a part of
our legacy, too

(114)

whether good or bad,
helpful or hurtful,
we will all leave a legacy
of one sort or another
when we die, and how
we remember others can
sometimes predict how
we, ourselves, will be
remembered, since it's
said that our friends are simply
mirrors for our true selves.


make an effort to acknowledge,
and be grateful for,
the influence of others,
and to recognize their legacy
as valued, because without
all of those beings who have
shared your journey with you,
you wouldn't be the person
you are today,
for better or for worse...

(115)

(116)

# epilogue

∞

# personal
# influences
# &
# reflections

forever loved,
never forgotten...
thank you
for loving me,
and for
letting me love you

(118)

use the following pages to identify those who have personally influenced your life so far, those who have made you who you are today.

this can include parents, teachers, friends, pets..... any being that left a lasting impression on you.

while the list can include beings you don't actually know personally, like celebrities you admire, try to stay focused on those you interact with on a regular basis, those whose death would affect your life in real ways.

what would they leave you?
what would you never want to forget about them?
what are you most grateful to them for?

let them know......

(120)

then, if you're feeling brave, use the last page to write what you would like your own legacy to be, what you would like people to remember about you when you're gone.

decide what kind of influence you would like to have on others, and then go live your life in a way that ensures that happens!!

you only get this one go around in this body, so why not make it enjoyable for both yourself and for those you interact with?

with love, peacewillow

(122)

## personal influence #1

name-

relationship-

favorite memory of them-

influence they had on me-

why i'm grateful i knew them-

(123)

(124)

personal influence #2

name-

relationship-

favorite memory of them-

influence they had on me-

why i'm grateful i knew them-

(126)

personal influence #3

name-

relationship-

favorite memory of them-

influence they had on me-

why i'm grateful i knew them-

(128)

## personal influence #4

name-

relationship-

favorite memory of them-

influence they had on me-

why i'm grateful i knew them-

(130)

personal influence #5

name-

relationship-

favorite memory of them-

influence they had on me-

why i'm grateful i knew them-

(132)

## personal influence #6

name-

relationship-

favorite memory of them-

influence they had on me-

why i'm grateful i knew them-

(134)

personal influence #7

name-

relationship-

favorite memory of them-

influence they had on me-

why i'm grateful i knew them-

(136)

# personal legacy

name-
what i'd like others to remember
about me-


influence i'd like to have on:
friends & family-


coworkers/classmates-


pets/critters-


the world!!-


personal trait i am most grateful
to have-

(137)

www.ingramcontent.com/pod-product-compliance
Lightning Source LLC
Chambersburg PA
CBHW072155090426
42740CB00012B/2274